SOLOMON'S WORLD

Jake Wild Hall

PRESS

Solomon's World

Published by Bad Betty Press
www.badbettypress.com

Cover design by Joel Auterson

Printed and bound in the United Kingdom

A CIP record of this book is available from the British Library.

ISBN: 978-1-9997147-1-0

For Solomon

SOLOMON'S WORLD

"There is no romance in curtains that are never opened."

Joel Auterson

Jake Wild Hall is the winner of the 2016 Spirit of the PBH Free Fringe Award and a multiple slam champion. He hosts Boomerang Club, one of London's warmest and most well-loved poetry nights, which enjoyed a popular full run at the Edinburgh Fringe. He's performed at the Royal Albert Hall and opened for Daley and Afrikan Boy at the Lyric. His work has appeared in the London Spoken Word Anthology (GUG Press, 2016). Jake is a vegan chef who loves the combination of peanut butter and hot sauce, and the father of a boy named Solomon.

Contents

Delicate Cycle

It's funny how the sleep
is clockwork now,
steady
pattern
integrated
into brainwave
already.

Wake seven thirty.
Sleep seven thirty.

I don't remember tears
pulled
from the night's silence
so quickly,
it was more
fingers stuck in exhaustion,

smile flickers
between your presence,
nonexistence.
I wish
I could weave my name
through the threads
of your comfort

but the night time is your blanky.

It's funny how my sleep
is hard work now.
Tea stained,
pen pricked
pages
begin to fill,
steady.

Wake eleven thirty.
Sleep five thirty.

I'd like a presence
in your non-existence.
My exhaustion
quickly flickers
into the night's silence.
Tears I'll remember.

Wake eleven thirty.
Sleep eleven thirty.
Repeat.

Bottle

I wake every morning
curled into the shape of a bottle
and talk myself down off the cap.

"Dad, your room's a mess and there are no toys here."

He is not entirely wrong.
And he still asks to come here.
It helps that the room next door is a story
with mountains, rivers and monsters,
a tree-sized man
and a Pixie godmother.

They shape days into arcs
that have heroes
and villains.
They break for biscuits
and juice,

then take off for adventure
until sunsets come calling
and he rides off into them.

Tonic

Our whole story is a grave with no headstone,
just dead space and decay.

We burnt the home we had built in our hearts,
coughed up the ash to clear space
and every day that was
has to be forgotten.

Every story I ever write of us is dust.
Memories, punch drunk
pulled out by spirits
with little tonic.

System

The red light flashes.
I am not yet safe for access.

Right hand,
right pocket,
rummage,
nothing.
Left hand,
left pocket,
birthday badge,
Batman branded,
put in a tray
deemed a safe place.
I am four.
I don't think this
is a safe place
but I can tell by mum's face
today ain't no day to play games.

Mum walks in
heavy footed as always,
like she's walking through mud.
I want to run off
but it's not safe.

The café's light catches my eye.
Quick check of mum's face.
Definitely not the right time or place.

His posture is a red light.
The creek of our chairs
hangs in the air.
It tastes like unwelcome news.
We hug,
I feel not much.
Like I know I won't have to save a place
at Christmas or my birthday again.
Mum checks my face,
she knows what I know.

Snow

It's three in the morning
          eleven where you call home.

We stand in the snow
          a joy home never brought you.

Your smile
        is the most beautiful thing
                    you run back and forth
a ball on a string
                    you make tracks
you are endless energy and we|are melting into each
other
        you scrape sentiment off a car
                and throw it at me.

Zip Up

In the morning
as *you walk streets*
littered by last night's
attempts to salvage some
sobriety for the walk home
you will know it's colder
as you zip up hoody
holding in the heat
of *a heart beating*
much louder than
you are used to.
Happiness and
love are often
impossible
to accept
like *cold,*
but *you*
zip up.

Space

Dad's jokes would sometimes knock the laughs
right out of me.
Not so much
rib tickling,
more held in the air I lost
from my gasp,
breathe in.
My mum was the same,
like the heat from the Florida sun,
the dry air hits you.
You readjust,
the laugh slips out
and grows into a fit.
I always said they should film you two.
You'd respond, *no one would laugh like you*
but I wasn't born with this laugh.
You taught me this.
Now we cut time together
with the same burning comments.
We drink coffee in the mornings
and whiskey by night,
wrap our darkest moments in sarcasm.

We are wine-stained stories
but you are still life lessons.
I still tie myself to your good will
and though this year is a photo taken in space,
we will laugh again.

Giants

At the edge of the world you will find giants,
is what they used to say
and they were not far wrong.
When you reach the edge,
all that will reflect are demons.
The ones you created for yourself.
They'll ask you one thing:
Are you ready?
You know this to mean jump
and you will stand, balancing on the edge,
too burdened by the weight,
knowing that a step forward
would be absolute.
Until you discover the world is round,
the morning you wake up
spitting distance from an angel
who will make you believe
in heaven again.*

---

* <u>Twelve hours earlier:</u> *Would you like a drink? - Ok, let's go on an adventure.* Electro swing tent. Dance. Kiss. To the tents. To the stages. *If the truth be told I'm a sucker for the high grade.*

72 hours later
you have gone 24 hours, no weed
and woken up in a bed
you will learn to call home.
This is where you start.[†]
Three weeks later
this romance is already three cities
and two countries wide.
We stand on a bridge and watch fireworks.
It couldn't get more poetic than this
but we're poets and we give it a try.
I wish I had told you
you made my world round again
but all I could wrap my tongue around
was what I knew to be true.
I love you and I think
this is where we start.

[†] <u>Adventure notes:</u> Sexual Healing. Jurassic 5. *That is an AT-AT walker.* Horizon.

Pixie

I go to catch my breath
and you already have one hand on it.
The other flicks the kettle on,
you make a brew only magic could have made.
How did you find a way
to fill this empty space?
It's not like me and you are playing games.
This is not for love-finding sake.
Been known to say *I love you* too much
but when it comes to *I need you* I don't say it enough.
But it's easy with you.
I need you.
I need you a lot.

Full

Sharing the air
with the poison-dipped sword
you aim at your heart,
I bite my tongue
and taste tears.

The blank hospital walls say too much
but I can't say enough.
My words are too easily pinned up
as an attack on you.
I am not attacking you.

I don't let you see how you hurt me.
I've already seen you burn
your closest loved ones' tears for energy.

I brought a plate full of sorrow
to every dinner table.

When I brought it to yours
you refused to let me go
until I had taken a bite.

Strange, how full your plate is.

Hold Me

I know our numbness is a pin drop
in the middle of conversation.
Our tissues are soaked in salt.
My brief visits are a pale attempt at support
and we are both looking down
because you are at the end of a world
that created you.

When I stop by, I know the kettle being on
is one step from *hold me*
like you did the first time,
before a plaster and a kiss on the cheek
was the answer to any knock life brought.
Before two arms meant *change*
or *feed*
or *save me from these dreams,*
when *hold me* meant
we're in this for nine months.
Make me ready for my first breath.

My premature release must feel
like I have miscarried your love.
A week later, pneumonia will save us
from funerals. I still won't sleep,
knowing when our joint path looks too bleak,

I will retreat.
My roots are weathered.
I've been forgetting how to be settled for years,
waiting for home to find me
but the weather is calming and *home*
is a word that, again, fits in my mouth.
I find myself at two compass points.
I want to share that with you
and I think I remember how you like your tea.

Soya,
no sugar
and with a hug.

Solomon's World

I have woken up three times this week. Same dream. Same restless sleep. Same three and a half you I wake up to. Question filled, full for dinner, but not for pudding, mother's side eye learnt well. You giver of umbrellas to rainbows. You who learn first lessons under roofs made of treetops. Your potential is a galaxy.

When I dream, I dream of you. I dream that we are living in a war zone and for you, today is the first day war broke and my skin is a bulletproof vest I cannot give you. Up until today, I could answer all your questions, but today your footsteps were a threat. Your posture was a man wielding a knife. You are thirteen, how do I tell you, you are still sunshine?

Question one: *Why did they stop me, dad?* The day you realise you cannot relate to your son's anguish, your thought process will be a bridge. Your shoes will be made of concrete and you realise you still have no trouble catching a taxi. So you lie: *It was a mistake, son. Wrong place, wrong time.* This distrust will make your relationship a maze you find yourself in again and again.

Question two: *Why did they call me that, dad?* The day abuse rolls off your white privileged skin and hits your son in the face like a sock full of coins, that maze will become a labyrinth and only in the centre can you find the answers, so you dance around them, enchanted by the patterns in the markings until questions now he's hardly asking. Because you never provide the answers.

Then you wake, shaking, mind racing because right now you're digesting all his unanswered questions. I think tomorrow I will take him to the park, wearing hope like a band-aid I know will fall off one day.

But right now I'm back to being tongue-tied. His footsteps are back to being sunshine. On the way home, I give him a shoulder ride. *Hey son, life is like a fun fair ride. It has its ups and downs but when you get off, I'll always try to be by your side. Your record will sk–sk–skip beats, but I'll help you back in the groove. Oh and your potential really is a galaxy, while mine has become a planet.*

He looks down. *Dad, I am three and a half years old. I don't think this makes any sense.* And we laugh together. But I still dream. Deep in the thought of the unknown.

Question three: *Why do people treat us different?* My thought process is still a bridge, but it's one I hope we can walk together. Although I'll never truly understand what he's put through, I will try to. And I hope everyone wakes up from this nightmare the same way I do, and realises equality is a branch on this tree of life we are yet to reach.

Acknowledgements

To all the people who have taken time to look over my poetry at any point.

In particular, I am very grateful for the input of Amy Acre, Hannah Chutzpah and Joel Auterson.

To my parents, grandparents and uncle Peter for their undying support and enthusiasm.

To those who have caught me with their couches and love when I thought all was lost, and the ones who told me to keep writing: Celeste Veazey, Max and Maya Frank, Jack Fontaine, Shannon Denny, Harry Wills, Harry Baker, Will Sanderson-Thwaite, Daisy Thurston-Gent, Tyrone Lewis, Caz Ann Moy, Maria Ferguson, Peter DeGraft-Johnson, Holly Holston and John Breslin.

And to Dean Atta, Deanna Rodger and Jenna Omeltschenko, who made an artist of me.

Lightning Source UK Ltd.
Milton Keynes UK
UKHW011535291219
356066UK00002B/115/P